AF664582

better together*

* This book is best read together, grownup and kid.

akidsco.com

a
kids
book
about

a kids book about MENTORS

by Josh Shipp

A Kids Book About
Editor Emma Wolf
Head of Design Rick DeLucco
Publisher Jelani Memory

DK
Senior Production Editor Jennifer Murray
Senior Production Controller Louise Minihane
Managing Editor Hazel Eriksson
Publishing Director Mark Searle

This American Edition, 2026
Published in the United States by DK Publishing,
a Division of Penguin Random House LLC
1745 Broadway, 20th Floor, New York, NY 10019

Text and design copyright © 2026 by A Kids Book About, Inc.
'A Kids Book About' is a trademark of Dorling Kindersley Ltd.
'Kids Are Ready' and the colophon 'a' are trademarks of A Kids Co.
26 27 28 29 10 9 8 7 6 5 4 3 2 1
001—356889—Aug/26

All rights reserved. Without limiting the rights under the copyright reserved above, no part of this publication may be reproduced, stored in or introduced into a retrieval system, or transmitted, in any form, or by any means (electronic, mechanical, photocopying, recording, or otherwise), without the prior written permission of the copyright owner.

No part of this publication may be used or reproduced in any manner for the purpose of training artificial intelligence technologies or systems. In accordance with Article 4(3) of the DSM Directive 2019/790, DK expressly reserves this work from the text and data mining exception.

First published in Great Britain in 2026 by
Dorling Kindersley Limited, 20 Vauxhall Bridge Road, London SW1V 2SA
A Penguin Random House Company

The authorised representative in the EEA is
Dorling Kindersley Verlag GmbH. Arnulfstr. 124, 80636 Munich, Germany

A CIP catalogue record for this book is available from the British Library

ISBN 978-0-2417-9493-7

DK books are available at special discounts when purchased in bulk for sales promotions, premiums, fund-raising, or educational use. For details, contact: DK Publishing Special Markets, 1745 Broadway, 20th Floor, New York, NY 10019, or SpecialSales@dk.com

Printed and bound in China

www.dk.com

akidsco.com

Interested in bringing Josh Shipp to your school or event?
Visit topyouthspeakers.com

MIX
Paper | Supporting responsible forestry
FSC www.fsc.org
FSC™ C018179

This book was made with Forest Stewardship Council™ certified paper – one small step in DK's commitment to a sustainable future.
Learn more at www.dk.com/uk/information/sustainability

To the countless mentors who have shaped
my life—Gary, Mrs. Dilbeck, Mr. Andrews,
Dr. Smith, Coach Wilson, Jamie, Sam, Rhett,
Mr. Colley, Patsy, Kirk, Goff, Kern, Hawk,
Bobby, Craig, Ramsey, Tuesday Night Inc.,
and so many others—THANK YOU!

Intro
for grownups

Mentors changed my life. I wouldn't be here without them. And I don't mean one, magical, mythical mentor who had all the answers. (No such thing.) I'm just talking about one caring adult after another.

And then another.

And then another.

Each one who helped me take the next small step forward.

That's what mentors do.

This book will help the kid in your life find mentors of their own.

And remind them they already have a few in their midst.

Including you. 👊

What's a B

G dream you have?

Have you ever dreamed of being...

A FAMOUS YOUTUBER?

THE BEST PLAYER
ON YOUR TEAM?

A REALLY LOYAL
FRIEND?

Howdy, I’m Josh.

And when I was a kid,

my big dream was to play baseball for the Texas Rangers.

DREAMS ARE AWESOME!

But we cannot reach them alone.

Every dream, major or small,
needs a squad of mentors.

MENTORS

are grownups who help you
level up a part of your life.

And you need mentors—plural—
because no one person is
awesome at everything.

(Myself included.)

When I was a kid in foster care,
life felt confusing and often scary.

But one caring adult after
another helped when I asked.

Not by accident or by luck.

But because I asked mentors for help.

THEY TAUGHT ME
HOW TO THROW
A BASEBALL,

SAVE MY
LAWN-MOWING
MONEY,

AND FIND THE
COURAGE TO SPEAK
UP FOR MYSELF.

I am who I am today because
of the mentors in my life.

So, how do you go about getting your own squad of mentors?

BEHOLD my legendary, patented

MENTORSHIP MAP™

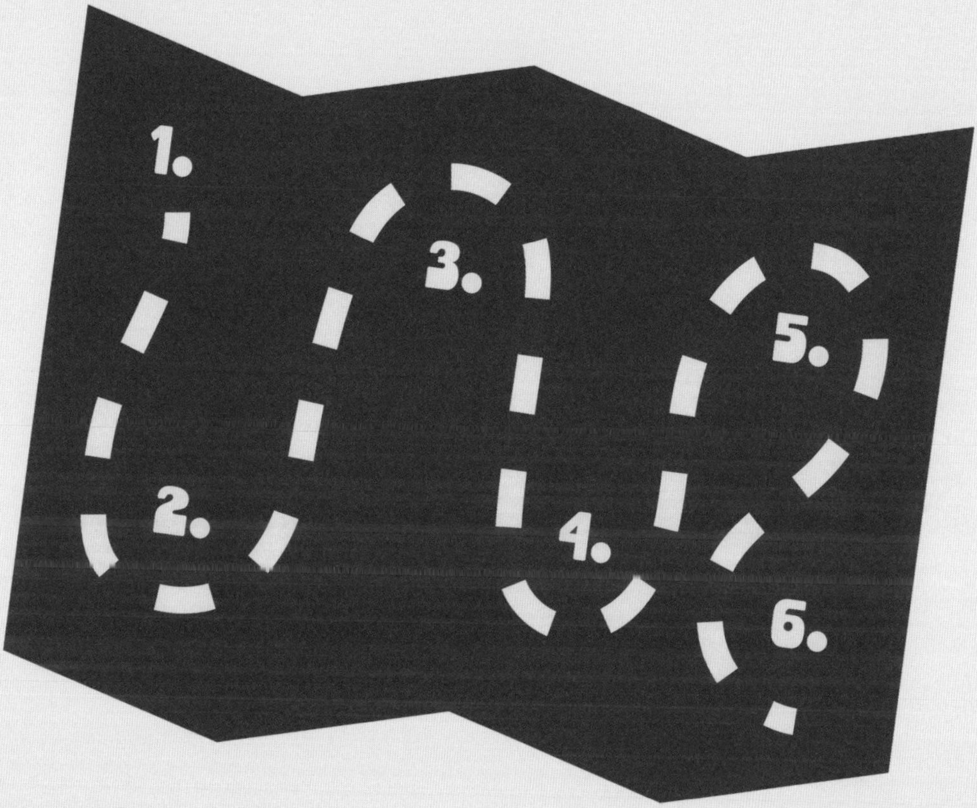

These are the six steps to get mentors who will help you succeed.

STEP 1:
PICK ONE THING.

CHOOSE ONE PART OF YOUR LIFE YOU WANT TO IMPROVE.

Don’t take on everything at once; start small.

It could be...

making friends,

getting better at a sport,

growing sharper math skills,

building confidence,

becoming a stronger public speaker,

or being kinder.

Your call.

STEP 2:
BRAINSTORM
5 NAMES.

THINK OF 5 POSSIBLE MENTORS WITH A TRUSTED GROWNUP.

There's a good chance the mentors you need are already in your life—you may just not think of them as mentors.

Maybe it's your favorite teacher
or coach, or a grandparent.

Who's good at that thing you
want to get better at?

WRITE DOWN

THEIR NAMES.

STEP 3:
ASK UNTIL YOU GET A YES.

GO DOWN YOUR LIST, AND ASK EACH PERSON UNTIL ONE OF THEM AGREES TO MEET WITH YOU.

This might feel scary, awkward, or intimidating.

TOTALLY

NORMAL.

Rehearse asking with
your trusted grownup first.

You will feel more confident.

Ask on the phone, through email or text, or even in person.

Need a little help with what to say? Check out *The Get-a-Yes Guide* at the back of the book.

STEP 4:
MEET WITH YOUR MENTOR!

GET TOGETHER WITH YOUR MENTOR—AND BRING A NOTEBOOK.

Y’all can meet in person or online—either works just fine.

Make sure to ask,

"WHAT'S ONE SMALL STEP I COULD TRY THIS WEEK?"

THEN WR

THEIR

TE DOWN ANSWER!

Ain't no way you'll remember all their brilliance without notes!

Not sure what else to ask? Check out *The Meet With Your Mentor Guide* at the back of the book.

STEP 5:
TRY IT OUT!

IT'S TIME TO PUT THEIR BRILLIANT ADVICE INTO ACTION.

Remember that one small step your mentor suggested?

GIVE IT A GO!

Don't wait! Use the excitement of that meeting to get started.

Sometimes it'll go well,
sometimes not so well.
Either way, you're learning.

Don't be afraid to try
more than once.

It takes practice (and failure)
to build a new skill.

STEP 6:
MEET AGAIN.

LET YOUR MENTOR KNOW HOW IT WENT WITH THAT ONE SMALL STEP.

Thank them for their time
and share how it went.

Tell them what worked,
and what didn't.

Try asking, "What could I do differently next time?"

Looking for more good questions? Check out *The Meet Again Guide* at the back of the book.

BEHOLD!

You've now experienced the life-changing power of mentors!

Repeat steps 4 (Meet), 5 (Try), and 6 (Meet Again) to keep it going.

But remember, this is *A Kids Book About Mentors*—plural—not just one mentor.

As you grow up, you'll discover new parts of your life you want a new mentor for.

And one day, maybe you'll be a mentor, too!

I never played baseball for the Texas Rangers, but I know how to throw a baseball, thanks to Coach Wilson.

And I learned how to save my lawn-mowing money...thanks to Gary.

And I have the courage to speak up for myself...thanks to Mrs. Dilbeck.

Dreams are reached step by step, mentor by mentor.

Whatever your dream, mentors will show you the way.

THAT'S THE POWER OF MENTORS.

THE GET-A-YES GUIDE

REHEARSE WITH A TRUSTED GROWNUP

Hi ________ (MENTOR NAME), I'm ________ (YOUR NAME), ________ (YOUR AGE).

IF YOU HAVE A CONNECTION:

________ (EX. MY TEACHER), told me you're really good at ________ (ONE CATEGORY).

IF YOU DON'T HAVE A CONNECTION:

I really admire how you're good at ________ (ONE CATEGORY).

I'm trying to get better at ________ (ONE CATEGORY) and could use some advice.

May I please ask you 3 quick questions sometime—by email, online, or in person?

Thank you,

____
YOUR NAME

THE MEET WITH YOUR MENTOR GUIDE

HELPFUL QUESTIONS TO ASK YOUR MENTOR

When you were my age, how did you get better at ______________?
(ONE CATEGORY)

What's one common mistake people make in ______________, and how can I avoid it?
(ONE CATEGORY)

What's one small step I could try this week to get a little better?

THE MEET AGAIN GUIDE

MORE HELPFUL QUESTIONS TO ASK YOUR MENTOR

Thank you for the gift of your time and advice. I learned a lot.

When I tried ________ (ADVICE), I ran into ______________ (SPECIFIC STRUGGLE).

Could I get your thoughts on how to handle that better?

What do you think I missed?

Would it be okay if I report back after I try again?

Outro
for grownups

Investing time with a kid, like reading this book together, is mentorship. Thank you. I mean that. It's a big deal.

Now, let's help that kid put MENTORS into action.

Ask these questions to spark action:

1. What's one area of your life you want to grow in?
2. Who do you already know that's great at that?
3. Let's pick a day. What day will you ask them for 15 minutes?

Then stay in the loop. Ask what they learned, and how it made them feel.

Mentors (including you) can change a kid's life.

They certainly changed mine.

About The Author

Josh Shipp is a former foster kid turned youth advocate and award-winning keynote speaker. Featured by *Oprah*, *The New York Times*, and *Good Morning America*, Josh has become one of the nation's leading voices for youth empowerment and education. As the founder of Top Youth Speakers—a premier agency representing world-class speakers—he helps schools and organizations inspire the next generation and the adults who support them. Through his speaking, writing, and mentorship, Josh continues to champion the idea that every young person deserves guidance, encouragement, and the right mentors to help them take their next step forward. Learn more at TopYouthSpeakers.com.

Made to empower.

Discover more at akidsco.com